T0128279

OTHER BOOKS BY THIS AUTHOR

The Christmas Story
Step into Scripture
A Bible Study for Advent

Seder to Sunday
Step into Scripture
A Bible Study for Easter

The Book on Bullies
Break Free in Forty (40 minutes or 40 days)
Includes Forty Devotionals to Fortify Your Soul

The Book on Bullies
How to Handle Them without Becoming One of Them

AFTER EASTER

STEP INTO SCRIPTURE

A BIBLE STUDY OF THE FIRST ACTS OF THE APOSTLES

STEP INTO SCRIPTURE BIBLE STUDY SERIES

SUSAN K. BOYD

WESTBOW
PRESS®
A DIVISION OF THOMAS NELSON
& ZONDERVAN

WestBow Press books may be ordered through booksellers or by contacting:

WestBow Press
A Division of Thomas Nelson & Zondervan
1663 Liberty Drive
Bloomington, IN 47403
www.westbowpress.com
844-714-3454

ISBN: 978-1-6642-0878-0 (sc)
ISBN: 978-1-6642-0879-7 (hc)
ISBN: 978-1-6642-0877-3 (e)

Library of Congress Control Number: 2020919994

Print information available on the last page.

WestBow Press rev. date: 12/02/2020

To the reader who wants to know what happened after Jesus's resurrection, and is curious enough to step into the pages of the Bible, with a little imagination, and be part of the events that unfolded so long ago.

CONTENTS

PREFACE

Welcome to *After Easter*, the third study in the Step into Scripture Bible Study Series! Each study can be done separately or back to back. This series is inspired by the belief that Bible study should be as exciting today as watching a 3-D or Imax movie or being involved in a virtual reality video experience! The Step into Scripture Bible Study Series is created as an intriguing and different method of studying the Bible.

After Easter—Step into Scripture is written in the present tense, allowing you to insert yourself into the pages of your Bible and walk with historical biblical figures. As you take part in the action, you'll be able to decide what you think, feel, and do as events unfold. Scripture doesn't change, but you might. You have the opportunity to participate and interact with the study in each question as you step through this hole in time.

Seder to Sunday—Step into Scripture, A Bible Study for Easter was the first study in this Bible study series. It ended with you and the other disciples listening intently to Jesus as he disappeared in front of your eyes on the evening of His resurrection. Your thought on the last question of the final lesson of that study was, "What happens now?" This new study, *After Easter—Step into Scripture*, is the answer to that question. It is the first acts of the apostles.

After Easter—Step into Scripture was written to capture the thrill of spending time with the risen Savior, then experiencing how to live for him without seeing him.

Christ unexpectedly appears for weeks after his resurrection. He teaches and trains you and the other disciples who have followed him these last few years. While you are wondering when he will appear, there he is—on the shore of the Lake of Galilee, in a crowded room behind closed doors, or taking you to the Mount of Olives where he finally ascends into the clouds right before your eyes.

But now Jesus stops making appearances, having left you and your friends with the daunting task of evangelizing the world! But this is a Roman world full of dangers. Rome dominates and rules, but it isn't the only oppressor; your own religious rulers see you as a threat. They crucified Christ, hoping his ideas would die with him. But just as Jesus is resurrected, so new life is being poured into his band of loyal disciples. And you are one of them.

What is it like after being flogged and thrown in prison to experience an angel leading you out to freedom right under the guards' noses?

How excited are you at Pentecost when the wind

moves through the crowd, flames of fire dance above your heads and thousands of people come to Christ after one message preached by Peter? Are you amazed, frightened, empowered, or eager for what happens next?

After Easter—Step into Scripture is a Bible study that marks powerful beginnings for the new church, for the world, and for you. Enjoy this study as you step into history. Then step back to today with a new sense of purpose. Because, after all, the acts of Christ are not finished!

INTRODUCTION

Have you ever wondered what it would have been like to walk and talk with the resurrected Jesus? Can you picture yourself being one of the apostles, trained by the risen Christ and then never being able to see him again (Acts 1:11)?

Imagine being one of the first people with the responsibility to tell the world that Jesus is alive and is the Son of God, especially to those who just crucified him (Acts 5:29–32)? This, the *Great Commission,* was one *great big* job (Luke 24:45–49)!

You can play an important role in spreading the gospel in *After Easter—Step into Scripture, A Bible Study of the First Acts of the Apostles.* As an interactive Bible study, it can be your personal journey with Christ or done in a group setting. Every part of this Bible study is meant to bring Scripture to life.

You will read a section called **Scene** that sets the stage and helps you picture the setting more vividly. **Note** sections are there for historical background and additional information to give Scriptures a context. **Note** sections are the only sections not written in the present tense.

The Bible study will occasionally direct you (especially in the scenes), suggesting thoughts or feelings you could be experiencing. But you ultimately decide what you think, feel, and do in any of the Bible study questions. If you are studying in a group, don't skip the **Scene** and **Note** sections. Read these all aloud together to get the full experience.

Pictures are placed before and after each lesson, making the Bible passages more visual for the reader. Poems follow each lesson to reinforce the content in that Scripture lesson or as an application for today. Again, avoid the temptation to skip past these. They are intentional and meant to bring you closer to the action, drama and truth of Scripture! Read them aloud together.

If you are doing this study in a group, listen to others' points of view as no answer is wrong if based on Scripture. Give everyone an opportunity to share. Try to complete the week's lesson before you meet together.

Each question has the verses supplied for you in order to answer that question. If you, however, want additional Scriptures and a more in-depth study, look up the passages under the chapter headings, and in the **Note** and **Scene** sections. *Do just one or two questions each day.* The lesson will mean much more if you take personal time to study before coming together to share insights.

Pray before you study each day, and the Lord will give you His perspective. He was there when the events took place and is with you now as you delve into Scripture.

After Easter—Step into Scripture is your chance to time travel to an exciting place with spectacular events in biblical history. The world today is full of impressive, visual effects. Let the Lord introduce you to some of his! Miracles are God's specialty.

As you step down deep into the Bible, you may step back to today changed. The Word has a way of doing that!

"For the Word of God is alive and active, sharper than any double-edged sword, it penetrates even to the dividing of soul and spirit, joints and marrow; it judges the thoughts and attitudes of the heart" (Hebrews 4:12).

A NOTE FROM THE AUTHOR

I wrote *After Easter* to give you a chance to step in at the beginning—after Christ's resurrection and before Paul's conversion.

You will experience what it was like to be the first to share the gospel and the last to see Jesus. You will be there to share the good news; salvation is found in no one else, for there is no other name under heaven given to mankind by which we must be saved (Acts 4:12). This is love on a grand scale, yet it is also a very personal message for everyone, including you—then and now.

THE SAVIOR'S LOVE

Thank you, Lord,
For not leaving the cross,
Believing I could be worth
That terrible cost.

You are nailed down,
So, I can be free.
In the request to forgive them,
You are thinking of me.

You could leave me,
Go back to heaven today!
No pain. No Lamb slain.
No sin taken away.

What makes a crucifixion, Lord,
Worth going through?
I hear a whisper in my ear,
"You."

BELIEVING WITHOUT SEEING: A LESSON FOR THOMAS

JOHN 20:24–31

Scene

The door opens. You and your friends (other disciples) file quickly into the room. You grab each other by the arm, give the customary kiss on the cheek, and slap one another on the back, greeting each other with wide smiles. The room's atmosphere is soon filled with the sound of excited voices. Everyone is talking about the details of your shared experience.

One week ago, today, it happened; your teacher, Jesus, who was crucified, dead, and buried, appeared in front of you all in this very room—alive!

The only person here without a story to share of that momentous day is Thomas, one of the original twelve Jesus chose as his disciple. Quietly brooding in the corner, Thomas frowns at every detail he hears.

1

You and your friends are retelling your stories of last Sunday, when Jesus came back to life! Everyone shares their favorite memory: the men who were taught prophecy from Scripture by Jesus on the road to Emmaus (Luke 24:13–32); the disciples who talked with him in this house (John 20:19–20); Mary Magdalene who saw him outside the tomb, (John 20:11–16); the women who peered into an empty tomb and then saw angels (Luke 24:4–7) and finally encountered Jesus himself (Matthew 28:8–10)!

For Thomas, the most difficult account to hear is possibly that of Peter, who apparently had a private interview with Jesus (Luke 24:34)! Thomas hears each report, one after another, as nothing more than a wild, hopeful imagining. He can't believe any of it because he didn't see any of it.

Thomas wasn't with you that day. He didn't witness the shock and disbelief on *your* face the night when Jesus, out of nowhere, appeared at dinner. The doors were locked. But *he* was here!

The Savior, seeing everyone's terrified expression, asked for cooked fish to eat so no one would think he was a ghost (Luke 24:36–43).

You closely watched Jesus chew and swallow each bite of food in front of you! Your risen Lord invited you and the other disciples to examine and handle his wounds.

Jesus turned his hands over where you saw the

giant, jagged crucifixion nail prints deep in his palms, close to his wrists. As he turned his hands again, you observed the same on the back of his hands (Luke 24:39). His feet had similar large gashes from the huge spikes thrust through the top of each foot. An exit wound could be seen at the back of both heel bones.

You saw no beaten, swollen face or torn flesh from the flogging or crown of thorns that once marred the appearance of Jesus. He had to point out his injuries to all of you (Luke 24:40). The only remaining proof of all he had been through was the evidence of the crucifixion itself. Jesus looked perfect except for these awful wounds that weren't wet or bleeding but were not old scars either (Luke 24:41). They were fresh punctures showing traumatized flesh on a whole and well body.

You understand why all this information is difficult for Thomas to take in, but you're a little insulted that he doubts all of your testimonies. You have traveled and ministered together for almost three years. You wonder, *Can't he take my word for it? Why is he elevating himself to be the judicial critic and making me out to be the gullible, naïve student of the departed rabbi?*

But Thomas may be misunderstood by all of you. And you notice his disgruntled expression gradually turning to sadness. The more everyone relays details of how they felt in the risen Christ's presence, the more stricken he appears.

Now you begin to feel sorry for Thomas. You think, *He's grieving the loss of our rabbi and friend. And he wasn't able to be here to see him on the most important day of all.* You think, *Maybe Thomas is wondering, "If Jesus is alive, why did he not wait until I could be here too?"*

Step back to a time in the past to answer questions 1–4. Examine closer the years of ministry and relationship Thomas had with Jesus.

1. Jesus had many followers he taught and sent out to evangelize and do miraculous deeds (Luke 10:1–22). These were known as his disciples. How did Jesus decide which disciples (to be known as the twelve disciples and designated as apostles) would be in his inner circle (Luke 6:12–16)?

2. Note: Thomas was also called Didymus, which in Aramaic and in Greek means "twin," though his sibling is unknown in Scripture (John 11:16). Read Thomas's experience in the story of Lazarus, the man Jesus would raise from the dead. How

would you describe Thomas's personality and his relationship with Jesus (John 11:1–16)?

3. Jesus tried to prepare the twelve for his death and ultimately his return to his heavenly Father. How does Thomas's question show his pragmatism as well as his devotion (John 14:1–6)?

Step back to this room, with Thomas and the other disciples for the following questions.

Note

The well-known title of Doubting Thomas originated from this disciple's skepticism regarding the resurrection of Christ.

4. What does Thomas say to you and what conditions does he give God before he will believe Jesus is alive (John 20:24–25)?

5. What do you notice listening to Thomas and watching his body language? Does he seem angry, sad, or just confused?

6. Why do you think Jesus waited a week before reappearing (John 20:26)?

7. How do the words of Jesus remind Thomas and you that he hears your words and knows your concerns whether you can see him or not (John 20:26–27)? How could that help you and the others in the future?

8. Who is Jesus talking about when he says, "Blessed are those who have not seen yet have believed" (John 20:29)?

9. This is a three-part question.

When Jesus reappears what does Thomas call him
(John 20:28)?

Do you see Thomas ever touch the hands and side
of the risen Christ as he had earlier insisted, he
must do?

What do you see and hear as Jesus holds out his
hands to Thomas? Describe this scene and your
own reaction to seeing Jesus again.

10. Who does Jesus say is more blessed, Thomas who
saw the proof of the risen body of Jesus or those
who will choose to believe without the physical

proof (John 20:29; 1 Peter 1:8–9)? Note: The word blessed can be translated to happy.

Note

Tradition has it that Thomas, the disciple of Jesus, went on to eventually evangelize India and Parthia![1]

11. Step out of Scripture and come back to today for this question. This is a three-part question.

Do you relate with Thomas and struggle with your own doubts? Which doubts are the most difficult for you to overcome?

What physical evidence or proofs have you needed or do you need in order to believe Jesus is alive?

List them here and try not to edit yourself. (As seen in this first lesson, the Lord can handle your doubts.)

Has Jesus ever shown you that he hears your words, knows your concerns, and sees you even when you can't see him? How do you know? One example might be answered prayer. If so, what were some of the details of that experience?

THOMAS'S TWIN

Lord, sometimes, I feel like Thomas,
The disciple who felt left behind,
Wondering where you are today.
Do I need to see you to ease my mind?

Why is having faith so difficult for some
And doubting so easy to do?
Never wanting to be the skeptic,
All I ever wanted was you.

Thomas was loyal, dedicated,
With concerns and a stubborn pride.
You gave him a week to ask himself,
"Do I need to touch his hands and side?"

Maybe as Thomas and I in the waiting,
Give up demands of proof or a show,
We'll each withdraw our hand, fully understand,
What our hearts already know.

GOING FISHING WITHOUT JESUS: A LESSON FOR PETER

JOHN 21

Note

Jesus gave direction to his disciples before his crucifixion regarding where they could see him after his resurrection. He stated, "After I am raised, I will go before you to Galilee" (Matthew 26:32). An angel told the women at the empty tomb, "Then go quickly and tell his disciples: 'He has risen from the dead and is going ahead of you into Galilee. There you will see him.' Now I have told you" (Matthew 28:7). As the women hurried away from the tomb Jesus himself met them with, "Greetings! Do not be afraid. Go and tell My brethren to go to Galilee; there they will see Me" (Matthew 28:9–10).

Some confusion may come from reading in the Luke 24 passage, Jesus told his disciples to wait in

Jerusalem until they were "clothed with power from on high" (Luke 24:49). So, which were they to do—meet him in Galilee or wait for the power of the Holy Spirit in Jerusalem?

The answer comes in understanding that the instructions found in the last verses, 44–49, could very well have been given at a different time than the previous verses in Luke 24 (Luke 24:1–43). Luke gives no indication (as he did in the preceding verses) that this particular command to wait in Jerusalem, was told to them on the first day of the week (Luke 24:1).[1]

Similarly, verses 50–53, describing Christ's ascension, actually referred to the forty days after Christ's resurrection. Yet they follow these same verses in chapter 24 of Luke as if the ascension were the next event to happen (Luke 24:50–53). By reading each of the gospels with the book of Acts, a clearer picture can be seen of all Christ's appearances though not an exacting timeline.

Peter and the other disciples had every reason to leave Jerusalem and venture out to Galilee. They had been told on different occasions that Jesus would meet them there. But where in Galilee? And when? How long should they wait? Patience was never a virtue of Peter's (Matthew 16:21–23; Matthew 17:3–5; Matthew 18:21–22; John 18:10–11), James's or John's (Mark 3:17; Mark 10:35–40, Luke 9:52–56). And Thomas, certainly, did not want to miss seeing Jesus again! He had enough of waiting (John 20:25)!

Scene

You, Peter, and the disciples travel seventy miles from Jerusalem to Galilee.[2] Jesus does not appear— you are waiting and wondering.

1. This is a two-part question.

   Are all the disciples together with you on the shore (John 21:1–2)?

   How many decide to go fishing on the Lake of Galilee (John 21:1–3)?

2. This is a three-part question.

   Does Peter ask anyone to go with him?

Who decides to go (John 21:1–3)?
(Note: The two other disciples are not mentioned by name. Though disciples of Jesus, they may or may not have been of the original Twelve.)

Why do you want to fish rather than wait on shore or somewhere else?

3. What had been the profession of Peter, James, and John before they became disciples of Jesus (Matthew 4:18–22)?

Note

Israel's largest freshwater lake, Lake Tiberias, is known as the Sea of Tiberias, Lake of Gennesaret, Lake Kinneret, and the Sea of Galilee.[3] Peter, James, and

John were back home! Peter probably commandeered his own fishing boat that still sat on the beach in their hometown.

Possibly, in the three young men's absence, Zebedee (James and John's father), had been using Peter's boat along with his own boats to continue their joint fishing business (Luke 5:10). The Galilean disciples may have piled into Peter's boat and then sailed across the lake to a more remote area to fish.

4. How long are you out on the lake, and how many fish have you caught (John 21:3)?

5. This is a three-part question.

   Dawn is breaking. A stranger on the shore calls out in the direction of your boat. By what familiar term does he refer to you (John 21:4–5), and what does he ask you?

What advice does the man on shore offer (John 21:6)?

Describe all you remember of a catch not long ago, much like today's, as you struggle to pull up the heavy net almost bursting with fish (John 21:6; Luke 5:4–11)? What striking comparisons do you make?

Scene

Stopping your work, you stand straight up in the boat and look intently at the man who is walking on the shore. As he watches you and your friends, you recognize the broad smile across his face.

Everyone aboard the vessel is laughing as they frantically shout orders to one another, "Pull! Pull! Don't stop. Help me lift. They are everywhere! Heave! Don't let any get away. The net is breaking! Don't let it break! John, get down here and help. What are you both looking at?"

You and John have been staring, riveted on the familiar figure on shore. You can't take your eyes off of *him*.

Looking down, you and John see the overwhelming job your friends are tackling! The net is so full they can't hoist it into the boat. No one wants to lose this valuable catch! You both grab-hold and heave the net bulging with fish. But even with everyone working, you can't lift the bulky, heavy load out of the water over the side into the boat.

John looks over his shoulder at the man watching you from the shore. Finally, John grabs hold of Peter's arm. He emphatically tells Peter exactly what he and you have been thinking the last few minutes.

6. What are you and John realizing that Peter has not noticed until now (John 21:7)?

7. Which are you doing—diving into the water with Peter or pulling in the net with John and the others (John 21:7–9)? Why? (Note: Many Bible scholars believe the phrase "the disciple whom

Jesus loved," written by John, may have been a reference to himself without divulging his own name [John 21:7]. This did not mean he was loved more, but that he felt confident in his relationship with Jesus.)

Scene

Peter swims to shore. Now on his feet, he walks straight to Jesus. Peter's robe hangs on him, heavy and wet. Before swimming, the disciple threw on his outer garment (John 21:7). You grinned, thinking, *He must not want to greet Messiah bare-chested in a loin cloth that he wore to go fishing!*

Back on the beach, Peter wipes water out of his eyes to see more clearly the man in front of him. He shakes his head, smiling. Jesus smiles back and then looks past him. He's watching you, John, Nathanael, Thomas, and the others laboring to get the boat to shore.

The net overflowing with fish is tied up, hanging from the back of the boat. You and Nathanael have been holding tight to the net to keep it from breaking loose. Though you weren't far out, the others dig deep with oars to bring the boat and its heavy cargo, being towed behind, into shore (John 21:8).

As you land you see your risen Savior standing on the beach! Behind him, fish are barbequing over burning coals (John 21:9). All of you leap out of the boat, quickly walk and then sit by the fire with Jesus and Peter. Everyone is silent. And not a man can take his eyes away from the Lord's. This is almost as exciting as the night of his resurrection! Suddenly, Jesus says, "Bring some of the fish you have just caught" (John 21:10).

Before anyone can move Peter runs to the boat, climbs in, unties the net and drags it to shore (John 21:11).

The rest of you get up and walk over to the beach, squat down and begin sorting and counting fish. None of you have seen a catch like this since the Lord last took you fishing!

Then unexpectedly you are looking up into the face of Christ. He invites all of you, "Come and have breakfast" (John 21:12). You follow him back to the fire and wait for him to speak. Instead he begins serving each of you!

Everyone is awestruck to be so close to the Lord once again. All of you watch Jesus work over the fire.

The Master reaches out handing you bread and his barbecued fish to eat (John 21:13). Then Jesus hands bread and fish to Peter and the others. Embarrassed, you look at Peter, now realizing, even though Jesus had directed you, no one brought even one of your *many* fish to add to his meal! You are still trying to wrap your mind around the fact that the risen Messiah is here, cooking you breakfast on the shore!

After this meal with Jesus, some of your friends go back to the rows of fish they had been sorting and counting on the beach. They look over at Jesus and announce the number, as if he didn't know! They say it over and over again to each other as they laugh out loud together.

8. How many fish did you catch this morning (John 21:11)? The proceeds from the sale of these fish will go a long way to support and feed all of you, your families, and anyone needing help.

9. Jesus doesn't inquire why you were fishing and you don't ask him who he is. What do you imagine this breakfast together is all about (John 21:12–14)?

Note

Some commentators through the years have noted that when Jesus asked if Peter loved him, the first two times he used the word for love which is a sacrificial, unselfish love, the type God demonstrates (John 21:15–16).[4] When Peter answered back, he used the word for love that means affection or brotherly love (John 21:15–16). The third and final time Jesus asked Peter, he used Peter's word for love asking if then Peter loved him with a brotherly love (John 21:17). Somewhat saddened by the repeated question, Peter answered "Lord, you know all things; you know that I love you" (John 21:17). Peter once again used the word describing a brotherly love.

In Jesus's three questions of love and his three commands of duty, that meant to tend, to herd, and to lead to pasture, Greek synonyms are used. Therefore, since it is difficult to see any consistent distinctions that John intended, most Bible scholars see these as stylistic variations.[5]

But whether Jesus and Peter used different variations of the word *love* or not, Jesus had his reasons for drawing attention to that word for Peter's sake and that of his friends as they sat by the fire.

10. This is a three-part question.

You listen closely as Jesus asks three times if Peter loves him (John 21:15–17). Describe memories you have of Peter and the night of Jesus's arrest. (Matthew 26:33–35, 69–75). What do these questions now, have to do with Peter's boast and denials then?

As you sit listening, do you think Jesus is reinstating Peter and his leadership, giving him another chance, or directing him on what he expects—any, all of these or something else (John 21:15–19)?

How do you think Peter is feeling right now? Describe the expression you see on his face as Jesus keeps asking him the same question (John 21:17).

11. Who are Jesus's sheep (John 10:1–18, 21:15–17)?

12. Do you think Jesus is giving Peter back a leadership position as well as including you and the others to watch over the *sheep* (John 21:15–17)? What are your thoughts as you watch and listen to Jesus and Peter?

13. How is Peter being reminded to keep his focus on Christ instead of questioning God's plan for someone else's future (John 21:18–25)?

Note

John was the only apostle of the twelve who was possibly never martyred (except for Judas Iscariot, who committed suicide). John wrote the gospel of

John which emphasized the divinity of Christ more than any of the Synoptic gospels (Matthew, Mark and Luke). He also authored the epistles, John I, II, and III. He wrote Revelation, which God gave to him in a vision while exiled on the Island of Patmos.

Peter, the Rock on which Christ would build his church (Matthew 16:18), is thought by early church historians to have dictated a large portion of the book of Mark. Mark's gospel is regarded by many Bible scholars as the first gospel written. Peter may have given his eyewitness account to his companion Mark to record.[6]

Peter was one of the main pillars of the early church and leader of the twelve disciples. He wrote 1 Peter, letters for "God's elect, exiles scattered throughout the provinces of Pontus, Galatia, Cappadocia, Asia and Bithynia" (1 Peter 1:1) and 2 Peter.

Early church history records that Peter was executed in Rome after faithfully taking care of "the Lord's sheep."[7] As Jesus predicted (John 21:18–19), when Peter was old, with his hands stretched out, he would be led away to where he would not wish to go. Peter would then be crucified on a cross like the Lord he served. The answer to the question, "Do you love me?" (John 21:17) was a resounding yes.

14. Step out of Scripture and come back to today for this question. This is a three-part question.

Jesus had the fish caught and cooked when he helped his disciples make their best catch. What have you been waiting and looking for in your life that Christ has already provided?

How has Jesus shown you in this lesson that he never gives up on you? How does that help you today in your own life?

If you, like Peter, need to know you are forgiven and that God has a plan for your life, then what would your answer to Jesus be to the question given Peter, "Do you love me?"

GOING FISHING

JOHN 21

I said, "I am going fishing."
It's what I have always done.
I will search. I can work
Way past the setting sun!

In the morning—an empty net,
Then a voice from the shore
I've heard before
Said something I'll never forget.

"Friends, haven't you caught any fish?
Let your nets down on the right side of the boat."
We pulled in such an abundance of fish
My little vessel could barely float!

I knew this was my Savior.
He had done this once before.
He's still helping me, calling me,
Waiting on the shore.

I dive into the water,
Leaving behind the life I knew,
Lord Jesus, you already have what I need.
And all I need is you.

LESSON 3

APPEARING AND ASCENDING: LEADERSHIP TRAINING BY JESUS

MATTHEW 28:16-20; MARK 16:15-20; LUKE
24:44-53; JOHN 21:24-25; ACTS 1:1-11

Note

The gospel of Luke and the book of Acts were both written by the same author, Luke. He was a Greek physician who later traveled with Paul, documenting the apostle's missionary journeys.[1] Luke did his research from the accounts of many eyewitnesses, including himself (Luke 1:3).

Acts could be called Luke's second book. He was writing to Theophilus, in both the gospel of Luke and in Acts (also known as the Acts of the Apostles). Luke explained his purpose for giving such detailed accounts, "so that you may know the certainty of the things you have been taught" (Luke 1:4).

For forty days, the risen Christ appeared and trained his disciples for the tremendous work of evangelizing the world. He appeared unannounced and disappeared just as quietly. For over five weeks, Christ's followers never knew where or when he might join them.

The disciples were also attempting to understand that when Jesus was not visible, he was still there. They would need to believe in this new reality to carry them through the years ahead. Great opposition was about to mount against them—more than they could have possibly imagined. Their faith and God's invisible power would give them the confidence to accomplish this important work.

Scene

You and the other disciples are in Galilee when Jesus tells you to go to a mountain nearby. As you sit together there, some are questioning whether they have been actually witnessing Christ's appearances (Matthew 28:16–17).

You all dismissed the women's story when they shared their encounter with the resurrected Christ (Luke 24:9–11). Thomas certainly doubted for an entire week (John 20:25–27). So now you wonder if your desire for this to be true is overriding common sense? Is it really Jesus you are seeing and hearing between these long and short absences? That very moment Jesus stands next to you and hears your thoughts (Matthew 28:18).

Some of your friends begin to worship and praise Christ. But others reluctant and in disbelief, stare and listen, afraid to trust their own eyes and ears (Matthew 28:16–17).

1. What credentials or authority does Jesus have that may help you believe that he is from God and is God (Matthew 28:18–19)?

2. Describe the amazing assignment Christ is giving you and the other disciples on this mountain today (Mathew 28:19–20).

3. What personal promise does Jesus make and how is that encouraging you (Matthew 28:20)?

SUSAN K. BOYD

Scene

Days turn into weeks. You are spending more time with Jesus. As you're watching him eat, listening to him teach, sitting by a fire together or walking with him, doubt dissolves. You are happy and relieved when you see the Lord appearing to more of his followers. Women who were loyal to him (Matthew 20:20–21; Matthew 27:55–61; Luke 8:1–3) and men considered as disciples (though not chosen as the twelve) (Luke 10:1–23) come in droves as the word gets out that Christ is alive. Other faces are people you've never seen following Jesus until now.

To your astonishment, you see some temple priests in the crowd. They listen—their eyes fixed on Jesus. You wonder if they were the priests offering the evening sacrifice at three o'clock in the temple when Jesus declared from his cross, "It is finished" (John 19:30).

At three o'clock, as Jesus took his last breath on the cross (Mark 15:33–37), the heavy curtain separating the Holy of Holies from the Holy Place in the temple tore in two from top to bottom (Mark 15:37–38). For the first time, the Holy of Holies was open. If the priests were there, they saw it (Acts 6:7)!

Are these priests making the connection you're making? The torn curtain now allows entrance to the Holy of Holies for everyone, not just the high priest and not only on the Day of Atonement. And now Christ's torn flesh and life sacrifice opens the way to God the Father for everyone (Hebrews 10:19–23.) No more obstacles exist.

Looking around this afternoon, you wonder how many people are here. You and some others decide to count people as they sit on the Galilean hillside listening to Jesus teach about the kingdom. You and your friends share the total and come up with the same number—five hundred (1 Corinthians 15:5–6)!

You listen to the words of Jesus and look over the faces in this crowd. You're still taking it all in—the number of followers of the risen Savior is growing fast (1 Corinthians 15:3–8)!

Note

As the forty days come to a close, Jesus prepares the disciples for their leadership responsibilities.

4. During your time together Christ begins to teach you from the Scriptures once again. Which books is he quoting to prove he's the prophesied Messiah (Luke 24:44–46)?

5. List different aspects of the work Christ is entrusting to you and where it will begin (Luke 24:47–49).

6. What is the reason you are to wait in Jerusalem before beginning your ministry (Acts 1:4–5, 7–8; Luke 24:47–49)?

Note

The last day Jesus spent with his disciples was in Bethany (Luke 24:50–53; Acts 1:1–12). Leading them out himself, Jesus walked and talked with them until they all reached the Mount of Olives. (Luke 24:45–50; Acts 1:12). He used this opportunity to speak very intimately with his inner circle which were frequently still called the twelve. None of them could have known it would be the last time they would ever see him again.

7. Give the question your friends ask and the answer Jesus offers (Acts 1:6–8).

8. What one question, more than any other question, do you want to ask him now?

9. Will you ask Jesus your question? Why or why not?

10. Describe how you feel watching Jesus rise above the earth, moving away from you, higher and higher, finally hidden by a cloud, until you lose sight of him completely (Acts 1:9–12; Luke 24:50–53)?

11. This is a two-part question.

    How long will you stand there looking up for some glimpse of Jesus?

    What promise are the angels giving you as they challenge your perspective (Acts 1:10–11)?

12. Are you excited, sad, or both, even as you praise God for all he is about to do (Luke 24:50–53)?

13. Step out of Scripture and come back to today for this question. This is a four-part question.

    Is Scripture boring and confusing or becoming more exciting as the Lord opens your eyes as he did for his disciples? In what way is it boring or confusing and how is it becoming more exciting?

If you could see the risen Jesus now, what would you like to ask him or tell him?

For the next forty days, talk to Jesus during the day as you would to a friend. Read one verse from Scripture and sit for a few moments listening from the heart. Write in this space the questions you have for him and answers he may give you. Answers may come as simply a thought or impression as you reflect on each verse. Try to be open and frank.

If you are feeling alone or abandoned, what assurance do you need from God that he has not left you? Tell him exactly how you feel and what you need.

FOREVER WITH ME

Though I cannot see my Lord Jesus,
I believe he is always there.
By faith I can hear his heartbeat,
As he listens to my prayer.

LESSON 4

A NEW BEGINNING: A DISCIPLE IS CHOSEN; HOLY SPIRIT ARRIVES: PENTECOST!

ACTS 1:12–2:41

Note

The term *disciple* means to be a student of a particular teacher. Jesus had many disciples. However, the twelve (reduced to eleven) had been chosen out of all of the disciples to be Christ's inner circle.

This *inner circle* of Jesus's students were also Christ's representatives known as the apostles. The word *apostle* means "one sent out." It reflects a Hebrew word that refers to one acting as another's representative.[1] Some others in the future would also bear this title. Nevertheless, these were the pioneers of the faith!

All eleven of the original disciples (including the one they would add to make twelve again) were active in ministry. Three, however, took center stage. They were featured most prominently in the early acts of the apostles.

Peter, along with James and John (also known as the sons of Zebedee) appear to have begun where Christ left off. Though of the three, Peter and John are featured most often in the book of Acts. James is thought to have been the first or one of the first twelve to be martyred. During Jesus's earthly ministry, he took all three of these men aside for special instruction or to witness important events.

Peter, James, and John were taken by Jesus to the raising of Jairus's daughter (Luke 8:49–56) and to the transfiguration (Matthew 17:1–3). Later, they entered into the inner garden of Gethsemane as the Savior offered his prayer of agony and obedience before his crucifixion (Matthew 26:36–39).

These men had been honed for leadership. Now their metal would be tested.

Scene

After watching Jesus go up into the clouds, you and the other disciples walk back from the Mount of Olives to Jerusalem as instructed (Acts 1:9–12). You're thrilled over all that's happening. But you know you will not see your Lord again.

You and your friends walk back to the city and talk

about your first assignment, which is simply to wait. (Acts 1:4–8). But for what? The power of the Holy Spirit (Acts 1:8). But you wonder what this will look like and when the event will be. You try to imagine how you'll recognize this power. You walk upstairs to the large room where you and the disciples are staying (Acts 1:12–14).

Other followers of Jesus are gathered here today. Mary (Jesus's mother) and the women who have been devoted to Him (Acts 1:14) greet you. People are praying and talking together. You all tell them different bits of the story of Jesus going up into the heavens and about the power you're to wait for, here in Jerusalem. You relay the promise given by the angels after Jesus was out of sight. The small crowd becomes excited as they listen to your every word.

A familiar face in the group catches your eye—this is someone you never expected to see here. You know this person. He was *not* one of Jesus's supporters. He's a man whom you knew to be critical of Christ's ministry and at times intent on pulling him away from his work (Mark 3:20–21, 30–35; John 7:1–5). He is, however, someone who was close to Jesus. It's his own brother James (Acts 1:14)!

Then people tell you the news. After Jesus appeared to Peter, you, and the other apostles and the five hundred, he appeared to his brother James (1 Corinthians 15:4–7)!

Mary must have told her children about the prayer

meeting tonight. You notice another of Jesus's brothers here. He looks like Jude (Acts 1:14)! Apparently, like James, he may have had a change of heart. You remember how vocal all the brothers were in their opinions questioning the ministry of Jesus, their half-brother (John 7:1–5). You often wondered if this had hurt Jesus (Mark 6:4).

You notice Mary, the mother of Jesus, now sitting down beside John. You are recalling when Jesus spoke from the cross entrusting her into John's care (John 19:26–27). She had her own children. Yet Jesus knew they didn't at that time believe in Him. Now, however, at least one and maybe two sons understand what Mary carried in her heart all those years (Luke 2:19, 51).

Note: You could not have imagined that one day James would become the head of the church in Jerusalem and later write the book of James (Acts 15:1–29; Galatians 1:18–19; James 1:1).[2] Nor could you have guessed that in the future a letter would be written to believers bearing Jude's name.[3] He would strongly encourage followers of Jesus Christ to resist being led away by false teachers (Jude). You are marveling at God's grace.

Note

The phrase "in those days" (Acts 1:15) probably meant another point in time following the day of Christ's ascension.

The events during Pentecost may have taken place in an outdoor courtyard of a home or in a very large house of one of the more affluent believers—one hundred and twenty met there. This is a meeting to replace Judas and return the disciple number back to the original twelve.

1. What are the requirements for the man who will take Judas's place (Acts 1:15–22)?

2. Whose final approval are you and the apostles seeking in deciding between Mathias and Joseph (Acts 1:23–24)?

3. How are you and the others praying in order to find God's choice of the man who will be part of this apostolic ministry (Acts 1:24–26)?

Note

Pentecost is the seven-week period after Passover. It is also known as the Feast of Weeks, the Feast of Harvest, and the Feast of Firstfruits. The name Pentecost comes from the Greek word for fifty, but the Jewish name is Shavuot (meaning weeks or sevens).[4]

All Jewish men were to "go up," or make pilgrimage to Jerusalem for three of the most important festivals in their calendar year (Deuteronomy 16:16–17). The Hebrew word *aliyah* means "going up" and refers to journeying upward to the place where God put his holy name—Jerusalem.[5] One festival was Passover (Unleavened Bread), another the Festival of Booths (Festival of Tabernacles), and the third was the Feast of Weeks (Pentecost) (Exodus 23; 34; Leviticus 23).

Jesus appeared to his followers for forty days and then ascended back to heaven to sit at the right hand of God (Mark 16:19). The disciples couldn't have known when Jesus instructed them to wait in Jerusalem for the Holy Spirit to come on them (Acts 1:4–8) that their wait would be so short and the power would be so great and unmistakable (Acts 2:1–11)!

The word for *spirit* is related to the word translated "wind." It also means "breath." Both nouns—"spirit" and "wind" or "breath" are from the verb "to blow, to breathe."[6]

Scene

You and your friends are in Jerusalem celebrating the Feast of Weeks (Pentecost). Jerusalem is teeming with travelers who have come to celebrate this religious holiday.

All at once, you hear a sound like a gale-force wind. It comes straight down from heaven (Acts 2:1–2). Everyone is turning around trying to decide whether to run for cover or wait to see what is happening. Suddenly, flames of fire twist and twirl flying around you. Then they break apart into tongues of fire, moving above your heads! They hover inches above you, fire hanging in midair (Acts 2:3–4)!

Abruptly and unexpectedly, you are filled with joy and elation as you begin praising God (Acts 2:4). Hearing the noise, pilgrims (God-fearing Jews) here to celebrate the holiday come running in and flood the room. No one can believe what they are seeing or hearing (Acts 2:5).

The Egyptian Jews in the crowd are grabbing each other by the arms and pointing at you. Their eyes grow wide as they look both ecstatic and anxious. They seem to be recognizing every word you are saying in their own native tongue! People from different countries are hearing you and the disciples praising God boldly in their national language (Acts 2:5–11).

You turn your head to view the flames dancing above the others. You imagine Jewish pilgrims from all the nations here today have the same question you do: Is this what Moses felt like when God appeared to him in the burning bush on Mt. Sinai (Exodus 3:1–17)?

The wind makes you think of everything you ever learned in synagogue about the spirit and breath of God!

The creation story in the Torah, recorded by Moses, told how God's Spirit hovered over the waters (Genesis 1:2). You wonder, *Was it anything like this?* Then God breathed into Adam's nostrils the breath of life (Genesis 2:7).

You ask yourself, *Was it such a short time ago Jesus, my risen Lord, breathed on me?* He said, "Receive the Holy Spirit" (John 20:22)! You are filled with wonder! You suddenly realize, *This same powerful Spirit of God is here today!*

4. Which distinguishable languages are the people hearing and understanding as the disciples begin to speak? Name all the different nationalities present and languages represented today (Acts 2:6–12).

5. How do you feel about what the critics are saying about you (Acts 2:13)?

6. How does Peter answer the accusation that you are drunk? Give the two proofs he gives in rebuttal: the time of day and the prophetic prediction (Acts 2:14–21).

7. Point out the highlights of Peter's moving sermon that you like best and why it's so compelling an argument (Acts 2:22–40).

8. How many converts are made today (Acts 2:40–41)?

9. Step out of Scripture and come back to today for this question. This is a three-part question.

    Have you ever been surprised by a boldness or courage God gave you in order to help others? Describe the situation.

Do you recall a time the Spirit empowered you to speak up in a way that you never thought you could? What happened?

Have you been ridiculed or misunderstood by others when you shared your faith in Jesus as the risen Christ? What was your reaction when criticized, and how could Peter's fearless rebuttal help you in the future?

MY PENTECOST

Lord God, your Holy Spirit
Lights the flame deep inside,
Burning into memory every word,
You gave me as your guide.

You warm me with your presence,
Like the comfort of a fire,
Embers of hope carried
Higher and higher.

Though no wind rushes around me,
No flames dance up above,
A wildfire of faith sweeps through my heart,
By the power of your love!

LESSON 5

THE NEW CHURCH: FELLOWSHIP AND MIRACLES IN CHRIST'S NAME

ACTS 2:42–3:26

1. List all the ways you see followers of Christ coming together since the coming of the Holy Spirit (Acts 2:42–47).

2. How are you and other believers becoming a community as well as an outreach to others?

3. When and why are John and Peter going up to the temple (Acts 3:1)?

4. What does the crippled man want from Peter and John and what do they offer him instead (Acts 3:1–7)?

5. How does the lame man demonstrate faith in the name of Jesus, giving God all the credit for the healing (Acts 3:6–8, 11)?

6. What do you like about this man? What do you see and hear?

7. Describe the reaction of the people in the temple recognizing the beggar and his radical healing (Acts 3:9–11).

Note

Some of the first acts of the apostles—teaching, healing, and their trials—took place in and around the temple. Knowing the history of the temple and picturing this important place can make it easier to step into these scenes.

The magnificent temple was the pride of Israel. The first was Solomon's temple, begun in 967 BC and completed in 960 BC and later destroyed by the Babylonians.

The second temple was built under the leadership of Zerubbabel and dedicated in 515 BC. The second temple stayed in its modest form of reconstruction for almost five hundred years until the Roman period. Then the Roman-appointed Judean king, Herod the Great restored it.[1]

The enormous temple reconstruction project Herod the Great began was later finished by his son. It was forty-six years into construction when Jesus visited the temple at his first Passover during his ministry. The elaborate and beautiful architecture was finally completed just seven years before the Romans destroyed it in AD 70.[2]

There is not enough room here to describe all the exquisite building materials used in refurbishing the temple. However, Josephus, the Jewish historian documented the artistry.

Josephus reported the grandeur of the giant white limestone walls of the temple, overlaid with plates of pure gold and gleaming in the sunlight. The amount of gold covering the white limestone has been debated by archeologists. But the fact that gold was applied is not in question. Jesus mentioned the gold on the temple, which stands as another historical reference (Matthew 23:16–17).

Josephus described a row of one hundred and sixty columns inside one cloister. Each giant marble column was so big around that three men with outstretched arms could circle it and join hands.[3]

Archaeological excavations unearthed evidence that the Temple Mount platform consisted of twenty-five acres.[4]

The life of the community and indeed the religious sacrifices and prayers took place in this temple, the heart of Israel itself. Josephus attested that during all the years of construction, no temple activities or sacrifices were interrupted.

Solomon's Porch and Colonnade at the temple in Jerusalem was the place where rabbis frequently sat to teach their students. Each scholar sat with his own disciples sitting in a semicircle at his feet.

Many of the prophecies about the coming Messiah were the high points of any rabbi's teaching. It was here among the beautiful marble columns that Peter began to give his second sermon. No doubt some of the teachers and scribes were in earshot of his words.

8. How does Peter use the beggar's new strong legs as evidence of the power of Jesus Christ (Acts 3:11–13, 16)?

9. What bold words does Peter use to both convict (Acts 3:13–15, 23) and comfort his audience (Acts 3:16–22, 24–26)?

Convict:

Comfort:

10. How is Peter appealing to them by referring to their forefathers? As you listen to him, what point do you think he is making to his fellow Jews (Acts 3:13, 18–22, 24–25)?

11. (Note: The word *repent* in the original language does not simply mean "to be remorseful," but includes changing one's mind or purpose then turning to go in a different direction.[5]) Why does Peter direct the people to repent? What direction had they gone, and where are they to turn now (Acts 3:19, 23, 26)?

12. Step out of Scripture and come back to today for this question. This a three-part question.

What do you do when someone on the street asks for money? This is a realistic and difficult situation today. Do you typically give money (even if the person has no disability)? Why or why not? Do you pray with or for that individual? Share your thoughts.

Name one thing you need to turn your back on today in order to turn to Christ for a new direction? How is Christ convicting and comforting you at the same time?

What has been the best part of going with Christ in a direction he wants to take you?

REPENT—
TO TURN AND GO A DIFFERENT DIRECTION

Lord,
When I move further from you
In my old rebellious way,
Turn me, keep turning me,
Until I see you and stay.

I like my blinders, my tunnel vision,
So that I can't see my sin.
Turn me, keep turning me,
Back to you again.

As you call me back from wandering,
You offer me a life so new,
I can't help but turn around,
And go with you.

PETER AND JOHN'S ARREST; THE SANHEDRIN'S DILEMMA

ACTS 4:1–22

Scene

Today is the most exciting day since Jesus left your sight! Seeing the Holy Spirit appear in tongues of fire was spectacular (Acts 2). But healing a man's paralyzed legs in Jesus's name and thousands becoming believers seem to be evidence that you and your friends have the power from the Holy Spirit that was promised you (Acts 1:8; 3)! You feel the momentum building for the kingdom of God. Your confidence is growing!

Note

The captain of the temple guard, responsible for law and order, was the chief of police. He was in the priestly line and second only to the high priest.[1]

Scene

You turn and notice the crowd part and people whispering as angry priests and the captain of the temple guard escort the Sadducees to where Peter and John are teaching. The religious rulers begin shouting and accusing them. But of what? Still shocked, you watch as the officials grab hold of Peter and John and drag them off to jail to await their trial the next day (Acts 4:1–4).

You begin to wonder— *How could this be happening after such an exciting and obvious episode of God's anointing work? One moment, great miracles take place, and the next his followers are taken into custody. Where is the power of the Holy Spirit now? How are we meant to know what to do and when to do it?*

Meanwhile, Jerusalem is buzzing with talk of Jesus Christ and not only about the miraculous healing but also of Peter's spectacular speech. And your numbers are growing. Followers now stand at five thousand strong (Acts 4:4)! You are hoping their presence at the trial or waiting outside the court might intimidate the Sanhedrin and influence their decision to be lenient with Peter and John.

Note

The Sanhedrin was a Jewish supreme court consisting of seventy-one, religious rulers (seventy members plus the high priest). The court adjudicated rulings on cases regarding religious laws, civil cases, and religious misconduct. They also made up laws.[2]

This body of the Sanhedrin was made up of elders, chief priests, and scribes.

A group called the Sadducees were majority members in the Sanhedrin. Sadducees were an old priestly aristocracy and wealthy land owners.[3] Many were relatives of Annas (the high priest emeritus) and Caiaphas (the current high priest and son-in-law of Annas).

Pharisees were the religious-ruling newcomers. They were more liberal than the Sadducees. And between these two groups, much conflict existed around religious interpretation of Scripture.

Sadducees were conservative and only believed in the first five books of the Bible, the Torah. They disregarded all other scripture. And since the resurrection was not in the Torah, they didn't believe in the resurrection of the dead.[4] They were zealots on the subject. They were, therefore, particularly offended when Peter spoke of the resurrection of Jesus.

1. Who presides over John and Peter's trial? Give their names or titles (Acts 4:5–6).

2. What questions are the officials asking, and what are the points in Peter's answer (Acts 4: 7–12)?

3. List some reasons that the judges unexpectedly find themselves "astonished at these ordinary men" (Acts 4:13–14). (You are overhearing them making comments to one another.)

4. What is your first thought as the Sanhedrin goes into closed session to come to their decision regarding Peter and John's fate (Acts 4:15).

Scene

As you and the other disciples wait for the final verdict and decision of the Sanhedrin, your heart begins to beat fast. You feel sick as you recall watching Annas and Caiaphas walk into the judgment hall.

You have dark memories of the trial of Jesus, by this same Sanhedrin, Annas and then Caiaphas presiding (John 18:13; Mark 14:53).

Flashbacks fill your mind of following Jesus as they arrested him. You waited outside for that verdict too (John 18:12–27). The trial took place in the middle of a cold night. You can still smell the scent of the fire and feel the fear that at any moment you could be taken next (John 18:18).

You and John waited outside for a glimpse of Jesus—across the courtyard from Peter (John 18:15–16). Peter, you vividly remember, warmed his hands

71

by the fire (Mark 14:54), almost rubbing elbows with soldiers and servants of the high priest (John 18:18). You guess he wanted to be as close to Jesus as possible without being noticed. And you all waited there.

You recall, that shocking Passover night, almost jumping out of your skin as you heard the violent blows from inside Caiaphas's palace. Temple guards hit Jesus over and over again with their fists (Mark 14:65). You now wonder, *How would this trial by these same men have any different outcome today? If they would judge Jesus who was sinless and hand him over to the Romans to be crucified, who was to stop them from doing the same to his followers?* But then you remind yourself, *Jesus was in control of his own fate* (Mark 8:31).

Other memories cross your mind and begin to bring you comfort. Jesus saved you more than once during a storm in the boat that all but capsized (Matthew 8:23–27; Matthew 14:22–33), and later in the garden, he stepped between you and the soldiers (John 18:1–9). Surely, now, no one but Jesus himself could save Peter and John. You cannot see your Lord, but you remind yourself —*He is here!*

5. You are impressed at Peter's address to the Sanhedrin today. How has God changed Peter's perspective and attitude from the early days when you first knew him (Matthew 16:21–25; Acts 4:10–13)?

6. What is the Sanhedrin's dilemma (Acts 4:14–17)?

7. As Peter and John walk out of the trial free men, what are you recalling Jesus once said of Simon Peter (Matthew 16:18)?

8. Who is giving Peter the power to make such a courageous stand for Jesus today (Acts 4:8)?

9. How is the Lord using the faith and joy of new believers to control the opposition (Acts 4:21–22)?

10. Step out of Scripture and come back to today for this question. This is a three-part question.

   Have you ever had bad experiences from the past that made you doubt God could help you in the future? What happened?

   Describe an experience, like Peter standing before the Sanhedrin, when you had the sense that God was giving you courage to stand up for him. Did you feel like your boldness was coming from you or from the Holy Spirit?

How is the fellowship and joy of other believers helping you in your life today, even when the opposition is the strongest?

THE HEALER

I praise you, Lord, for the healing
Of every broken place,
Not only a body but a life of confusion,
A crooked path set straight.

You are the great physician
Touching emotions with your hand,
Making us bold where we were timid,
Helping us make a stand.

There is no one like you, Lord,
Who makes miracles come true!
The great physician healing hearts
That now can worship you.

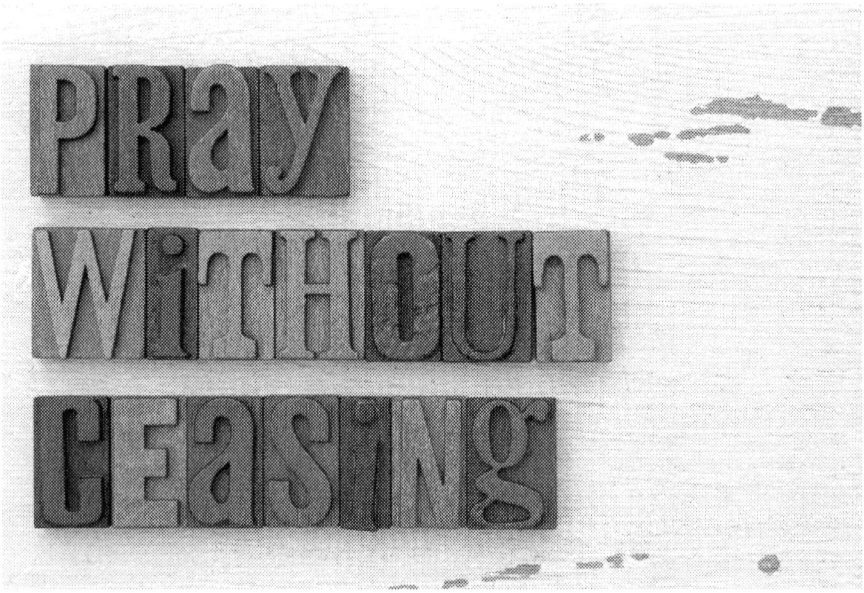
PRAY
WITHOUT
CEASING

THE HOLY SPIRIT'S FILLING; BARNABAS AND THE BELIEVERS' GENEROSITY

ACTS 4:23-37

1. Where did John and Peter go immediately upon their release (Acts 4:23)?

2. What is the response of the community of believers, and who is getting the credit for Peter and John's release (Acts 4:24–30)?

3. List and describe all the attributes and deeds for which you hear believers praising God today:

   God's sovereignty over the earth (Acts 4:24).

   The Holy Spirit inspiring David to prophesy about Messiah (the anointed one) (Acts 4:25–26).

   The trial of Jesus Christ and God's foreordained plan (Acts 4:27–28).

4. How are your friends inspiring you by not pleading for God's protection, as much as asking for boldness to speak and power to do more miracles in Christ's name (Acts 4:29–30)?

5. With all that has happened the last couple of days, what moves you most?

6. What event took place after you prayed these prayers together (Acts 4:31)?

7. Describe your friends and that which you appreciate most about all of them (Acts 4:32–35).

8. Where does the power and grace come from in such uplifting people (Acts 4:33)?

9. How do you see God working here (Acts 4:33–34) everyday? Explain.

10. Who is Joseph—this man who is becoming a prominent figure in your group? Where do you think he got his nickname, Barnabas (Acts 4:36–37)?

11. Step out of Scripture and come back to today for this question. This is a three-part question.

   Definition of miracle: A surprising and welcome event that is not explicable by natural or scientific laws and is therefore considered to be the work of a divine agent (lexico.com).

   Do you believe in miracles? Have you seen one?

Have you ever felt the power of the Holy Spirit and been moved by the realization of who God is?

How is the modern-day church like this early fellowship of believers, and how is it different?

TOGETHER

When together we praise you, Lord,
I wonder if you smile,
And close your eyes and listen
For a while.

When we help one another,
Does your heart overflow
With a joy because, finally,
We act on what we know?

Do you nod with satisfaction
When we glorify your name,
And we tell the world about your Son,
And why he came?

LESSON 8

ANANIAS AND SAPPHIRA LIE AND DIE; APOSTLES HEAL MANY

ACTS 5:1–16

Note

The followers of Christ began pulling together as a community of faith attending to one another's needs. Many sold property or items they owned and gave the money to the disciples (Acts 4:34–36). They were not forming a commune, nor were they establishing a communistic type of government of their own. The believers could keep that which was theirs, donate whatever they chose, whenever they wanted to do so.

Until chapter 5 in the book of Acts, the opposition to this new church was from the outside, mainly the religious rulers. But unknown to the band of believers, they faced a new enemy—this time from inside the church.

A married couple gave only part of the money they received from the sale of a plot of land to the church (Acts 5:1–2). They would, however, tell Peter they were giving *all* of their profits to God (Acts 5:2). People were no doubt impressed by the generous donation Barnabas had previously made. (Acts 4:36–37). Perhaps the husband and wife wanted the same admiration and attention from the church, for what appeared to be their sacrifice for the good of the whole.

Ananias and Sapphira were actually embezzling from the church by pretending all the proceeds from a land sale belonged to the fellowship when in fact, they were using part of it for themselves. The original verb for "held back" that Luke used to describe this action, actually meant, to "misappropriate."[1]

Therefore, it is likely that the couple had previously entered into a contract with the church to donate all the proceeds from the sale of the land.[2] And worse, they were lying, not to Peter but to God's Holy Spirit who had done so much for the church.

The greed and dishonesty of Ananias and Sapphira could have ruined the witness of how Christ's followers were to live. The outside world watched the church very closely (Acts 4:16). This was especially the case after the healing of the crippled man who praised God for healing him in the name of Jesus Christ of Nazareth (Acts 3).

The Holy Spirit had come in the form of fire, wind

(Acts 2), and miraculous events such as healing the crippled man. (Acts 3). The disciples boldly spoke out for Christ in the court of the Sanhedrin, by the filling and power of the Holy Spirit (Acts 4). The Spirit, however, as his name indicates, was and is forever holy.

The Holy Spirit was not to be taken lightly or underestimated. The fate of Ananias and Sapphira was not a result of making a mistake. They faced the consequences of lying to God and thinking they could get away with it.

1. Where did the lie begin and who was responsible for it (Acts 5:1–3)?

2. How do you think Peter knew the details of the plot Ananias had hatched and that Sapphira supported?

3. Exactly what was the sin of Ananias (Acts 5:4)?

4. Did Ananias confess or hold to his lie (Acts 5:4)?

5. What is your reaction as you hear about the two men's conversation and watch the body of Ananias get carried off, wrapped up, and buried (Acts 5:5–6)?

6. This is a three-part question.

    How does Peter give Sapphira the chance to confess and repent (Acts 5:7–9)?

    Does she take the opportunity to rethink her decision to continue the lie?

Why do you think both Ananias and Sapphira dropped dead when they were confronted (Acts 5:5, 10)?

7. This is a two-part question.

What is the reaction of the whole church and anyone who hears about the circumstances surrounding the death of Ananias and Sapphira? (Acts 5:10–11)?

Are you scared? Why or why not?

8. This is a two-part question.

What exciting events and conversions are going on at Solomon's Colonnade (in the temple) and out on the street (Acts 5:12–16)?

Describe all you are seeing and hearing!

9. This is a two-part question.

   More in the community are becoming believers.
   They continue to meet in the temple in Solomon's
   Colonnade. Others are reluctant to come.

   Explain the conflicted feelings people are having
   about your church (Acts 5: 12–16)?

   Are others fearful of Peter after the Ananias and
   Sapphira incident or are they afraid of the religious
   officials? What are your thoughts as you talk to
   people and observe those around you?

10. Step out of Scripture and come back to today for this question. This is a three-part question.

List the damage to the church in our society when people who call themselves Christians misuse church funds, lie, and deny their part in it.

How do non-Christians today view Christian leaders who turn a blind eye to wrong being done in the church?

The apostles taught the Word in the temple and helped people where their physical needs were— out on the street. Name some ways you would like God to begin or continue to use you to help others.

LIES—
LESSONS LEARNED FROM ANANIAS AND SAPPHIRA

Lord, I don't want to rationalize
My life away,
Fooling myself into thinking
Untruths are justifiable today.

How easily a word or deed
Becomes the compromise,
A good intention reduced to something,
I cannot recognize.

So, Lord, I will not try to impress,
Or think of what others see.
I'll simply offer myself to you.
That is all you ask of me.

AN ANGEL OF THE LORD FREES THE APOSTLES; THE APOSTLES KEEP TEACHING

ACTS 5:17–42

Note

1. Describe and contrast the reactions of the people being healed and those of the high priest and Sadducees. How are they different? What are you hearing and seeing? (Acts 5:14–17)?

2. What are the religious officials doing, and where are they taking you and the other disciples (Acts 5:18)?

3. As you sit imprisoned in the dark and cold tonight, knowing your trial is tomorrow, which words of Jesus do you suddenly recall (Mark 13:11; Luke 12:11)? How do the Lord's words from the past encourage you for the future?

4. This is a three-part question.

What other words of Jesus are you remembering this confusing and terrifying night (Matthew 10:28; 28:18–20; John 16:32–33)?

Before Jesus was arrested, he offered up a prayer to the Father on your behalf. You heard him pray for you aloud. Do any of his words have special meaning to you now (John 17:13–23)?

Do these memories help you or not? What else are you thinking tonight?

5. This is a three-part question.

    List the brief instructions the angel gives you (Acts 5:19–20).

    What is your first reaction as you leave the jail behind and walk through open doors (Acts 5:20–21)? List every thought that goes through your mind as you follow the angel past the guards. What sights, sounds, smells, and feelings do you notice?

Where are you going tonight? Are you sleeping on the temple steps or going home?

6. Describe the response of the officials and the scene the next morning as they frantically search for you and your friends (Acts 5:21–26).

7. This is a three-part question.

    Are you fearful or excited this morning, standing in the temple courts, telling the people about *this new life* (Acts 5: 20–21)?

    What is the *Way* and the *Life,* about which Jesus taught you (John 14:6)?

Which other teachings of Jesus do you want to share with those coming to hear you speak (Matthew 5:1–12; Luke 24:7; John 7:37–39; 14:10–13)?

8. As the trial begins, no one addresses the fact that an angel opened the jail door and you and the other apostles were found teaching in the temple at daybreak (Acts 5:19–21)! Why do you think the religious leaders avoid this subject?

9. Name the two accusations the high priest makes at your trial (Acts 5:27–28).

10. Give points in Peter's defense argument that explain why you and the other disciples are still teaching again today (Acts 5:29–32).

11. Identify the accusation Peter is making of this high priest and the exaltation he is proclaiming of Jesus as the Christ (Acts 5:30-32).

12. Which member of the Sanhedrin speaks up in your defense? Describe what you know about him by reputation (Acts 5:33–34)?

Note

Gamaliel was a scholarly, renowned, and beloved Pharisee. The Pharisees were more tolerant than their rival party, the Sadducees. Gamaliel was the grandson and follower of the liberal Rabbi Hillel. The Sanhedrin honored Gamaliel by calling him *Rabban*, or *our teacher*.[1] The second-century compendium of Jewish law called the Mishna says of him, "Since Rabban Gamaliel the elder died, there has been no more reverence for the law; and purity and abstinence died out at that time" (*Sotah* 9:15).[2]

As a Pharisee, Gamaliel believed that God was in control of everything happening, but he also believed in free will. He cautioned the Sanhedrin against exercising their free will in opposition to God's will.[3] Gamaliel was the teacher of the Pharisee Saul of Tarsus, who would one day be the well-known evangelist—the Apostle Paul (Acts 22:3).

Gamaliel spoke to the Sanhedrin when no apostles were present to hear. The question is—how did they know of his compelling speech? The details in his address to the court may have been relayed to the apostles by a member of the Sanhedrin who had converted secretly to Christianity. Two examples in the past were Joseph of Arimathea and Nicodemus (Luke 23: 50–56; John 3:1–36)). Another possibility is that Gamaliel told Saul, his student, who in turn later told the disciples once he became a Christian.

13. What logic does Gamaliel apply in his argument for releasing you and the other disciples (Acts 5:33-40)?

14. Which words in Scripture might they be recalling as they listen to Gamaliel's convincing summation (2 Chronicles 13:12)?

15. How are the Sanhedrin trying to dissuade you from telling others about Jesus (Acts 5:40)? (Note: this type of flogging was done with leather strips, typically thirteen lashes on the chest and twenty-six lashes on the back.[4])

16. What is keeping you from becoming discouraged after such a painful flogging (Acts 5:41; 1 Peter 4:12–14)?

17. Where are you going each day, and what are you doing (Acts 5:42)?

18. Step out of Scripture and come back to today for this question. This is a three-part question.

Have you ever had a miraculous rescue by God even though you may not have seen his angel? If so, describe what happened.

Can you remember a time you had to defend your faith in Jesus Christ? What did you say or what would you have liked to say?

What in particular brings you joy that can help put any pain and fear of persecution behind you? Make a list in order of importance.

BARS

Lord, nothing can hold me,
If you break open the door,
Not the darkest of dungeons,
Or a bottomless floor.

You pull back the enemy,
Blocking his plan.
You push aside trouble,
With a brush of your hand.

You saw me locked away.
I was never hidden from view.
You heard every prayer,
Which brought me to you!

LESSON 10

SEVEN DISCIPLES CHOSEN TO DISTRIBUTE FOOD; STEPHEN IS ARRESTED

ACTS 6:1–15

Scene

Every moment is more exciting than the one before. Miracles are a daily reality (Acts 5:12). Individuals who were lame are using their legs to get to prayer meetings (Acts 3:1–8). People once feared because they were demon possessed are now free of possession and friendly to those around them (Acts 5:14–16). Those previously blind open their eyes to a bright new world (Acts 5:16). They bring their neighbors to hear you teach (Acts 5:14). Many are becoming disciples of the Word (John 1; Acts 6:2). Lives are being changed.

You feel confident that you and the other apostles are in the process of doing the *Great Commission* your Lord handed to you before he ascended (Mathew 28:18–20).

SUSAN K. BOYD

All the apostles are starting to notice, however, that converts want more fellowship with one another. Your evangelistic efforts are creating a large community of believers (Acts 6:1). With this great success comes problems.

As the number of converts grow, you are gradually spending more of your time distributing food to those in need, like orphans, widows, and the poor. You find that less of your week is spent preaching as you face the logistical problem of managing people. You and the other apostles are also handling complaints.

Note

Jews who were natives of Palestine spoke primarily Aramaic; but Jews who lived in the Mediterranean world outside of Palestine spoke Greek and often did not know Aramaic.[1]

1. What complaints are the Hellenistic Jews bringing against the Hebraic Jews (Acts 6:1)?

2. Which people are you gathering together in order to communicate clearly the problem and the solution (Acts 6:1–3)?

Note

Acts 6:1–15 marks the beginning of the need for church structure.

For the gospel to spread, preaching and prayer were essential and needed the undivided attention of the twelve. Therefore, the apostles looked within the church for help with the needs of others. Individuals possessing both wisdom and maturity were chosen to take on these responsibilities.

Such leadership in a growing church meant people were needed who demonstrated sound judgment, fairness, and the use of gifts, including administration. The inclusion of women and different nationalities was also becoming more apparent.

3. How are you involving the faithful men and women in this decision process (Acts 6:3–4)?

4. What are the two criteria for the seven who will be chosen (Acts 6:3)?

5. (Note: All seven of those chosen had Greek names. The Hebraic-speaking Jews chose seven from the very group that issued the complaint.[2]) How did the church at large feel about this decision (Acts 6:5)?

6. Why do you need to turn this responsibility over to other gifted people? Is it because you think the work is beneath you or because it keeps you from doing your teaching and prayer ministry (Acts 6:2, 4, 6, John 13:12–17)?

Note

These seven men held new positions within the church that could be considered a forerunner to what is today known as a deacon. The word *deacon* is not, however, used here. Deacon means servant or "to serve or support" and later had the more common meaning of "to serve tables."[3] The twelve disciples had already been taught by Jesus the importance of serving (Luke 22:24–27; John 13:3–5).

7. How does laying on of hands and praying for the seven show your blessing and dependence on God (Acts 6:6)?

8. What is the result of God's blessing, the Holy Spirit, and the church working together (Acts 6:7)?

9. Step out of Scripture and come back to today for this question. This is a seven-part question.

   How did the Acts 6 church do the following, and how can today's church apply these principles?

   Complaints being promptly addressed by the leadership:

   Then

   Now

   Clear communication by the leadership to the church about decisions they are making:

   Then

   Now

   Involvement of the church members to help solve the problems:

   Then

   Now

Inclusion:

Then

Now

Trust:

Then

Now

Utilizing people's various gifts:

Then

Now

Priority placed on prayer and the ministry of the Word:

Then

Now

10. Stephen was one of the seven chosen to manage the distribution of food. He had the gift of administration. What were his other gifts and attributes (Acts 6:8)?

Note

The Synagogue of the Freedmen included individuals or their ancestors who had been set free from being slaves or prisoners of war. They came from three divergent groups: North Africa, Asia—the western portion of modern-day Turkey—and Cilicia (Acts 6:9). This may have been the assembly Saul of Tarsus attended, as Tarsus was located in the province of Cilicia.[4]

Some commentators take this passage as describing three synagogues. However, because the word *synagogue* is singular and not plural, other Bible scholars believe people from three areas (not three synagogues) joined the Synagogue of the Freedmen.

11. What does Stephen, the skilled debater, say and do that enrages the Jews at the Synagogue of the Freedmen (Acts 6:8–10)?

12. How does the opposition try to hurt Stephen when they cannot out-debate him (Acts 6:11–14)?

13. Describe the countenance of Stephen witnessed by every member of the Sanhedrin Court (Acts 6:15). What expression do you see on the faces of the Sanhedrin?

14. What are you seeing when you notice, Stephen's face is *like the face of an angel* (Acts 6:15)?

15. Step out of Scripture and come back to today for this question. This is a three-part question.

Do you like going to church? If not, why not? Make a list of reasons you do or don't care to attend.

Like going: Dislike going:

What gifts or talents of yours does the church need that you have been reluctant to use? Write down and share this list with someone who knows you well, or ask for input. Note: This is not boasting or being prideful. If you do not recognize you possess gifts, you will not know you have anything to contribute.

What do you think would help the church grow today?

In Spirit:

In numbers:

HIS CHURCH

Full of imperfect people,
With perfect gifts from above,
We give God the glory,
When we reflect His love.

As we each disciple others
By the Word and by deed,
People take heart when given a part,
Filling a need.

Inclusion means no one
Is left waiting outside the door,
The fallen and forgotten,
Are welcomed; restored.

We need strong voices,
Not reluctant to share *The Way,*
And eyes that look for the lost,
Every day.

THE FIRST BOOK OF MOSES,

CALLED

GENESIS.

e common Year of CHRIST, 4004.——Julian Period, 0710.——Cycle of the Sun, 0010.—
Cycle of the Moon, 0007——Indiction, 0005.——Creation from Tisri, 0001

CHAPTER I.

¹⁴ Of the sun, moon, and stars
²⁹ Also the appointment of food.

beginning ¹God created the heaven and

was without form, and void; and

upon the face of the deep: and the

moved upon the face of the waters.

said, ʰLet there be light: and there

that it was good; and

16 And God ʰmade tw
light † to rule the day, a
the night: he made ʰthe

17 And God set th
heaven to give light

18 And to ʰrule o
and to divide the li
saw that it was g

19 And the ev
fourth day.

20 ¶ And G
abundantly th

LESSON 11

THE SPEECH AND STONING OF STEPHEN

ACTS 7

Note

This speech given by Stephen is the longest message in Acts. Because of that, finding a thread that pulls this oration all together is helpful. The thread was the plan of the Almighty which ran through the life and history of Israel, and the knot was tied at the completion of his work through his son, Jesus Christ (Acts 7:1–53). The *Righteous One of Israel* was the Messiah the patriarchs looked for and whom this high priest and many of these same Sanhedrin crucified (Matthew 26:57, 59, 66; John 18:12–14; Acts 7:52–53).

Stephen never made a defense to accusations falsely lodged against him. He accused his accusers and his judges. He was brought up on two charges—speaking against the temple and the law (Acts 6:13–14). Stephen, in the time given him to make a case for his innocence, instead chose to give a history lesson to those well versed in the law (Acts 7).

Stephen's goal seems to have been to guide these learned men through their own shared history, to recognize that Jesus, not the temple, *held the presence of God and that Jesus, himself, was the fulfillment of the law.*

1. What impresses you about your friend Stephen (Acts 6:3; 6:8; 6:10; 6:15)?

   (Note: Besides the twelve apostles, Scripture brings Stephen and Phillip into the foreground as also demonstrating the ability to perform miracles, signs, and wonders through the power of the Holy Spirit (Acts 6:8; 8:5–7,13).

2. How does Stephen address the Sanhedrin (Acts 7:2)?

3. Why do you think Stephen never answers the charges made against him?

4. What promise did God give Abraham and his descendants (Acts 7:5)?

5. What impresses you as you listen to Stephen's understanding of Jewish history (Acts 7:6–8)?

6. Find similarities between the jealousy Joseph's brothers had of him and the jealousy the religious rulers have had of Jesus and his apostles (Matthew 27:17–18; Acts 5:17–18; Acts 7:9–16).

7. How do you see the sovereignty and timing of God as Stephen presents the well-known story of Moses (Acts 7:17–32)?

8. (The religious rulers held Moses in the highest esteem as their lawgiver.) Once again, how might Stephen be drawing a comparison between the Israelite's forefathers' rejection of Moses—who was *a type* of savior then—and the Sanhedrin's rejection of Jesus *the* true Savior, now (Acts 7:33–43)?

Note

The Temple, as alluded to earlier, was considered to be much more than a building. It was where the people of Israel believed God dwelt. Considered holy, Jews defended it fiercely, even against the occupying Romans. Jews were known to riot over Romans dishonoring the temple or Roman symbols or articles being placed anywhere on temple grounds or in the Holy City itself.

Scene

Stephen becomes more adamant as he closes his address. He educates his accusers about the true meaning of the temple, using historical references and the prophets' words.

9. Which words of Stephen's do you think challenge the religious rulers' understanding about God and his temple (Acts 7:44–50)?

Scene

Your friend Stephen seems more interested in preaching to the Sanhedrin and connecting the dots in history for them than trying to persuade for his acquittal. These men are scholars, and they know prophets from God in the past spoke with such fiery zeal. But you also know those prophets, who brought unwanted news were in many cases killed. Stephen never said he was a prophet, but without reservation he speaks out God's Word today!

You are amazed at the passion and conviction in Stephen's words! Now you realize what is happening!

You think— *He is more concerned about their souls than his own life.*

10. What does Stephen finally say, enraging the Sanhedrin, that convinces you he is about to receive the death sentence (Acts 7:51–54)?

Scene

You watch in horror as the now infuriated Sanhedrin have the temple guards drag Stephen outside. The religious rulers are cursing him through clenched teeth (Acts 7:54). The crowds that follow are gathering up rocks in their arms. You have never actually seen, close-up, a man stoned before, especially a friend. The scene is chaotic. Men are shouting and waving their arms.

You move a little farther away. You don't want to see the stoning, but you can't bring yourself to leave Stephen either. You begin to hope for the first time in your life that Roman soldiers will come around the corner so this will all stop!

Only Romans can legally administer capital punishment. But authorities are having difficulty keeping the peace these days and often won't interfere in local government affairs if religious officials are involved.

You can't see Stephen because of the huge crowd around him. Suddenly, everyone is quiet. They are making way for the Sanhedrin. The religious rulers peel off their official robes and drop them in a pile on the ground at a Pharisee's feet. He seems to be in charge of these garments during this execution (Acts 7:58). Each witness announces his name loudly and proudly.

Everyone is reaching down to pick up rocks. *Now* you can finally see Stephen! He is looking up with a serene smile. You have seen him like this before—he is clearly filled with the Holy Spirit (Acts 7:55)! To the Sanhedrin's shock, he begins to speak kindly, looking past his attackers as if he were seeing an old friend coming to get him. Choking back tears, you wish you were that friend.

Stephen points up to the sky; he gazes upward over the heads of his executioners. He looks surprised and elated. You think, *He must be actually seeing the glory of God* (Acts 7:55). His eyes glisten. He announces, "Look! I see heaven open and the Son of Man standing at the right hand of God" (Acts 7:55–56). At this, the Sanhedrin all cover their ears, screaming and shouting at the top of their lungs as they close in around him (Acts 7:57).

11. As the mob throws stones of every size at Stephen, you hear his amazing last words. How is his prayer similar to Christ's words from the cross (Luke 23:34, 46; Acts 7:59–60)? What happens after the prayer?

Scene

Stephen's pummeled body lies completely still on the ground. You are numb, unable to move yet. The Pharisee standing next to you picks up the robes of the Sanhedrin and hands them back as they each walk by (Acts 7:58). You had not looked at his face, until now. You recognize him. No one hates this new movement Stephen was part of or the idea of Jesus as Messiah more than this man. He has a reputation for being merciless with Christ's followers.

You think you overhear this Pharisee speak to one of the Sanhedrin members as he gives back his robe. You believe you are hearing him boast that he will soon be asking for papers from the high priest so he can go door to door and pull men and women that belong to *The Way* out of their homes and arrest them (Acts 9:1–2). You hear the hate and eagerness in his voice. It sounds as if he plans to take a delegation with him so he can imprison all followers of Jesus of Nazareth. He will be traveling to outlying towns and doing the same thing (Acts 9:2).

You are no longer paralyzed by sorrow but moved by a sense of urgency to tell Peter and the others of this danger. You turn and quickly scan the crowd for a familiar face. You know the other disciples are somewhere close by watching this. You put your head down, turn, and walk briskly up the road. You want to get away from this madman as quickly as possible before he becomes curious about you!

12. Who is this Pharisee (Acts 7:58)?

13. Step out of Scripture and come back to today for this question. This is a four-part question.

    Have you ever been required to go to court, or somewhere else, against your will? What was the worst part for you?

    When have you felt at the mercy of someone in power or authority?

    Have you ever felt the presence of God in a horrendous situation?

Describe a time the Holy Spirit empowered you to share Christ with someone because you were more concerned for them than worried about their reaction to you. What happened?

WHEN

Lord Jesus, *when* my time comes,
My work is done on earth,
When I look for a friendly face,
I hope yours will be the first!

I won't know the time or place.
You will make that choice.
I only want you to call my name,
And let me hear your voice.

When in those moments,
If you say, "You're not alone."
I'll know it's true—I've been with you.
Now, you will walk me home.

Lord Jesus, *when* I see your glory,
If you step toward me and say,
"You did what I put you here to do."
Lord, then I won't need to stay!

LESSON 12

SAUL THE PERSECUTOR; SIMON THE SORCERER; PHILIP AND THE ETHIOPIAN

ACTS 8-9:2

Scene

Until the stoning of Stephen, the church of Christ had been growing into a thriving community both in spiritual depth and in numbers (Acts 2:41, 47; 4:31-35, 5:14, 41–42, 6:1). But you knew the gospel was not leaving Jerusalem and the outlying areas.

Jesus had encouraged you with a prediction that had not yet been fully realized. "But you will receive power when the Holy Spirit comes on you; and you will be my witnesses in Jerusalem, and in all Judea and Samaria, and to the ends of the earth" (Acts 1:8).

After Stephen's public execution, the church was shaken. And now it is scared! Stephen had not been flogged and released as you were at your arrest and trial (Acts 5:40–41). Stephen became the first martyr for Christ (Acts 8:2). Church members are asking you, "Will we be next"?

Rumors are everywhere that believers of Jesus of Nazareth are being taken into custody (Acts 8:3). So, the church is scattering, trying to get as far from Jerusalem as possible (Acts 8:1). Some tell you they are going to relative's homes in other cities, while others want to disappear into the populations farther away. But you know they are taking the Gospel with them and preaching it wherever they land (Acts 8:4)!

Jews had through the generations journeyed to the temple in Jerusalem in order to worship God. The temple, however, is now every believer filled with God's own Holy Spirit (1 Corinthians 6:19). And all of them are *taking the* gospel from Jerusalem out into the world!

1. Who is back on the scene spearheading the hunt for followers of Christ (Acts 8:1–3)?

2. Why are you and the Apostles staying and keeping the Jerusalem church alive (though it will go underground) while others disperse (Acts 8:1)? Has this become the church headquarters?

Note

The Philip in chapter eight of Acts was a devoted disciple but not the same Philip of the chosen twelve (Luke 6:14). Philip was one of the seven Greek believers in the church in Jerusalem (along with Stephen) chosen to help distribute food (Acts 6:5).

As covered earlier, Philip and Stephen were two (besides the twelve disciples) who Scripture highlights in these early acts of the apostles as having supernatural powers by God (Acts 8:5–7).

3. How is Christ's mandate to, "Therefore go and make disciples of all nations, baptizing them in the name of the Father, of the Son and of the Holy Spirit," (Matthew 28:19) becoming a reality today (Acts 8:4)?

Scene

You have been traveling alongside Philip to Samaria (Acts 8:5). As he goes on into a city in Samaria, you stop briefly at Jacob's well. Resting in the heat of the afternoon, you draw refreshing cold water for yourself.

Your memories are sparked of being in this very place with Jesus (John 4:7). It was here at Jacob's well that you left Jesus to go into town with the other disciples to buy food (John 4:8). You came back with lunch and found Jesus talking with a Samaritan woman (John 4:1–38).

Jews never talked to Samaritans socially and certainly not to Samaritan women. But then, your Master broke lots of those rules! He brought down barriers.

You didn't know what Jesus said to the Samaritan woman, but she left her water pot and ran into town shouting to everyone who would listen, "Come and see the man who told me everything I ever did. Could this be the Messiah" (John 4:28–29)? Jesus, you and the other disciples stayed on for two days (John 4:40–41).

Jesus taught the eager Samaritans, who were excited not only because of what they were hearing from her, but from Jesus himself (John 4:39–43). Many became believers. You wonder if the people here are still as open to Christ.

4. Explain how the compassion of Jesus back then may be opening doors and hearts for the gospel now, as Philip addresses the Samaritans (John 4:25–43, Acts 8:4–8)).

5. Describe everything you hear and notice as God uses Philip and blesses the Samaritans (Acts 8:4–8).

6. As people talk to you about Simon the Sorcerer, what contrasts are you trying to help the Samaritans make between Simon and Philip (Acts 8:4–13):

   Promoting Christ verses promoting self:

Magic versus miracles:

Pursuit of Christ versus the pursuit of power:

7. Simon believed and was baptized. He is following you and Philip and seems extremely interested and impressed by the miracles. After watching and listening to him, what do you think Simon believes and wants (Acts 8:13)?

8. Give reasons you think the apostles at the church in Jerusalem are sending Peter and John to Samaria (Acts 8:14–17, 25).

9. Why was Simon not with the other believers, in your opinion, when Peter and John prayed and placed hands on them to receive the Holy Spirit (Acts 8:15–17)?

10. What enormous miscalculation is Simon the Sorcerer making, as he approaches Peter and John (Acts 8:18–24)? Describe everything you hear and see during Peter and Simon's conversation.

Note

Eusebius the church historian, one of the earliest writers to track the rise of Christianity, revealed information about Simon Magnus, who was, in his opinion, Simon the Sorcerer of Acts 8.

Simon the Sorcerer astounded people with his magic, and as Scripture reports, that he boasted he was someone great (Acts 8:9). Magnus promoted himself in the same way. Samaritans said of Simon the

Sorcerer, "This man is rightly called the Great Power of God" (Acts 8:10). The citizens of Rome, similarly impressed by Simon Magnus, erected a monument to him, worshipping him as a Deity. Both Simons were said to have had a following of people in high as well as low places (Acts 8:10).

Simon the Sorcerer tried to buy the Holy Spirit to impress people and add to his arsenal of power and illusions (Acts 8:18–19). Likewise, Simon Magnus used elaborate productions and amazed crowds with his spectacular feats of magic. Especially interesting is that Magnus was known to have mixed Christian beliefs with his own magic and twisted theology. If the two Simons were, indeed, one and the same man, this mixture of theologies may have followed Simon's brief encounter with Phillip the evangelist.

Many provocative stories about Simon Magnus have circulated throughout the years, some unsubstantiated. However, what is known is that his fame spread throughout not only Samaria, but also to other nations. Eusebius reported, however, that after Peter confronted Simon in Samaria, Simon quickly fled overseas.[1]

11. What are Peter and John doing for the Samaritans (Acts 8:15–17, 25)?

Note

The Samaritans did not receive the Holy Spirit when they first believed the gospel and were baptized. Why did two pillars of the church of Jesus Christ need to come from Jerusalem to Samaria to lay hands and pray for them to receive the Holy Spirit?

Many theories exist among theologians. However, John R. W. Stott gives what may be one of the best possible reasons:

"The most natural explanation of the delayed gift of the Spirit is that this was the first occasion on which the gospel had been proclaimed not only outside of Jerusalem but inside Samaria. This is clearly the importance of the occasion in Luke's unfolding story, since the Samaritans were a kind of a half-way house between Jews and Gentiles."[2]

Though Jesus had revealed himself as Messiah in Samaria, no one had been back to tell them of his crucifixion and resurrection. Jesus had shown compassion on these people who were part Jewish, and yet mixed Judaism with other religions, after the Assyrians had transplanted many foreigners there centuries earlier in their history.

Generations of animosity existed between Jews and Samaritans. Jews viewed Samaritans as the great pretenders, copying in part what they did not understand in whole. For example, conflict existed on subjects such as where God was to be worshipped (Jerusalem or at Mt. Gerizim—where a replica of the early Jerusalem temple had been built). Randall Price, the archeologist, in his book, *The Stones Cry Out*, cites an inscription found on the site of the temple at Gerizim from second-century B.C.; "The Samaritans adopted everything from the Jewish prayers to {their} sacrificial ritual."[3]

Religious bigotry had to be buried under a new foundation of faith, with Christ as the cornerstone. Jews and Samaritans needed to come to Christ for salvation. But they needed to come together for the sake of the unity of the church.

Stott points out, "At all events, the action of the apostles appears to have been effective. Henceforth, Jews and Samaritans were to be admitted into the Christian community without distinction. There was one body because there was one Spirit".[4]

12. How does Philip demonstrate his eagerness to be of help to God (Acts 8:26–32)?

Note

The Ethiopian eunuch was a man of great importance. He was in charge of the treasury of Kandake (Candace), the Queen of Ethiopia (Acts 8:27). Candace was a title given to the queen mother. Governmental power rested in the hands of Candace.[5]

The Ethiopian eunuch's position and wealth was evident in the fact that he was sitting in his chariot when Philip found him (Acts 8:28). The eunuch's attitude revealed a respect for God and Scripture. He had an intelligent curiosity. He was returning home after worshipping God in Jerusalem (Acts 8:27–28).

13. Trace Phillip's steps in assisting the Ethiopian eunuch (Acts 8:26–39):

Listening to and obeying the angel of God (Acts 8:26–29):

Looking for an opportunity to share the gospel (Acts 8:30):

Caring about the eunuch (Acts 8:30–38):

Knowing Scripture in order to help the eunuch understand it (Acts 8:32–35).

14. What was the result of Phillip's time spent with the Ethiopian eunuch (Acts 8: 36–38)?

15. What happened, following the baptism, when Phillip and the eunuch came out of the water (Acts 8:39–40)?

Note

After Philip left Gaza, he evangelized the cities along the Palestinian seaboard. He settled in Caesarea, which became the base for his evangelism. Twenty years later, still sharing the gospel, he was well-known as Phillip the Evangelist. He was also the father of four daughters with the gift of prophecy (Acts 21:8–9).[6]

Scene

You and the apostles have come a long way since the first week you tried to convince Thomas that Jesus was alive (John 20:24). Sometimes, you wondered yourself if Jesus were an apparition, and then, abruptly, he would appear again (Matthew 28:16–17). Forty unforgettable days with the risen Savior was the best time of your life (Acts 1:3)!

When you become discouraged, you recall the great catch of fish and realize you are indeed now fishers of men (Matthew 4:19; John 21). You are excited all over again, as you remember watching and listening to three thousand people in one day profess their faith from a single speech by Peter (Acts 2:41)!

Remembering the sight of flames over your heads and the sound of the mighty wind (Acts 2:1–4) encourages you that God is good for his word (Acts 1:4–5). And you know you will continue to experience the power on high when you need him most.

You are aware the persecution is intensifying; Jesus said this would happen (Matthew 10:22). But he also told Peter, "Take care of my sheep" (John 21:16). You and the other disciples did just that as you came to love the flock. You think of all those families that came together. So many were sharing with one another and praising God for all he was doing (Acts 4:32–36) even in the face of great opposition.

Now, new converts have a community of believers in Samaria (Acts 8:14)! They greet you with such enthusiasm for Christ. And this is just the beginning of taking the gospel beyond Jerusalem. And how many believers in another region might come from a freshly baptized eunuch, possessing a new understanding of Scripture?

Times are difficult, and you know you might be the next martyr. You smile, thinking, *They could not martyr Jesus though. He came into the world with the express purpose of dying for our sins* (Matthew 17:22–23; John 3:16). His love and sacrifice for the sins of his enemies as well as his friends is beyond anything you have known.

Your thoughts shift unexpectedly from praising God to the new threat on the horizon.

He is coming—the Pharisee who stood next to you at Stephen's stoning (Acts 7:58). He has one single, horrible mission—to destroy the church (Acts 8:3). You have heard he is on the road to Damascus right now (Acts 9:1–2).

You know the Pharisee must have received the papers from the Sanhedrin he requested (Acts 9:1–2). He is looking for you and your friends. But he will take anyone who professes Jesus as the Christ (Acts 8:2). Your Lord had said, "But I tell you, 'Love your enemies and pray for those who persecute you'" (Matthew 5:44).

So, you and the church are praying for the heart of the man who hates you the most. And you wonder if God could melt the iron heart of Saul of Tarsus and remold his life purpose. Then, the words of Jesus come back to you—"With God all things are possible" (Matthew 19:26).

AFTER EASTER

You and your disciples, Lord!
How exciting it must have been;
Eating, laughing, talking together,
They must have wished it would never end!

If I could sit and learn from you,
I would listen and never complain.
Asking questions that have burdened me,
I'd be reassured again.

Then, I open my Bible and begin to read.
You come to life in every word and line.
A righteous God who gave up his life
For mine.

I want the world to know you, Lord.
How can I help them to believe,
If you're not here to tell them?
Though, your Spirit *does* live in me!

"Then, child, remember, you take me with you
Everywhere you go.
So, share the Good News I have given you.
Let's tell them what you know!"

ACKNOWLEDGMENTS

I would like to extend my thanks and gratitude to Pastor Tracy and Pastor Rob. Both brilliant, insightful, and Godly men, they patiently listened and offered their advice. I thank the Lord for their wisdom!

I also want to express my appreciation to my dear friend Judi, who is a registered nurse. She helped me in understanding the physical condition of wounds, like those of the Lord Jesus. Her insight brought to light what the disciples might have been witnessing the night of Christ's resurrection.

NOTES

Lesson 1

1. Charles F. Pfeiffer, Howard F. Voss, John Rea, *Wycliffe Bible Encyclopedia, Vol.2* (Chicago: Moody Press, 1975), 1700.

Lesson 2

1. "To Galilee or Jerusalem?" Eric Lyons, M. Min., Apologetics Press, accessed Nov. 25, 2019, http://www.apologeticspress.com,
2. "New Testament Cities Distances in Ancient Israel," accessed Nov. 5, 2019, https://www.bible-history.com/map_jesus/MAPJESUSNew_Testament_cities_Distances.htm,
3. "Lake Tiberias (Sea of Galilee), Northern Israel," August 15, 2009, earthobservatory.nasa.gov, https://earthobservatory.nasa.gov/images/40147/lake-tiberias-sea-of-galilee-northern-israel.
4. H. A. Ironside, *Addresses on the Gospel of John* (Neptune, New Jersey: Loizeaux Brothers, Inc., 1984), 888–889.
5. John F. Walvoord and Roy B. Zuck, editors, *The Bible Knowledge Commentary; An Exposition of the Scriptures by Dallas Seminary Faculty, New Testament edition* (Wheaton: Victor Books, A Division of SP Publications, Inc., 1983), 345.
6. Eusebius, *Eusebius' Ecclesiastical History, trans.* C. F. Cruse, (Peabody, Massachusetts: Hendrickson Publishers, 1998), 50.

7. John Oakes, "What Is the Evidence That Peter Was Crucified Upside Down in Rome?" accessed March 20, 2020, evidenceforchristianity.org., https://evidenceforchristianity. org/what-is-the-evidence-that-peter-was-crucified-upside-down-in-rome/.

Lesson 3

1. Rey C. Stedman, *When the Church Was Young* (Palo Alto, CA: Discovery Foundation, 1989), 13.

Lesson 4

1. Lawrence O. Richards, *The Teachers Commentary* (USA, Canada, England: Victor *Book, A Division* of Scripture Press Publications Inc., 1987), 765.
2. "Was James Really the Brother of Jesus?" JB Cachilla, *Christianity Today*, April, 21, 2018, christianitytoday.com.
3. "What Happened to Jesus' Brothers?" Stephen Miller, *Christianity Today*, accessed April 3, 2020, christianitytoday.com
4. "Shavuot: The Feast of Weeks or Firstfruits," jewsforjesus. org., accessed Dec. 10, 2019, https://www.jewsforjesus.org.
5. David Brickner, *Christ in the Feast of Tabernacles* (Chicago: Moody Publishers, 2006), 16.
6. John F. Walvoord and Roy B. Zuck, editors, *The Bible Knowledge Commentary*, 357.

Lesson 5

1. Randall Price, *The Stones Cry Out: What Archeology Reveals About the Truth of the Bible* (Eugene, Oregon: Harvest House Publishers, 1997), 177.

2. "Construction and Rebuilding (Herod's Temple)," accessed March 29, 2020, bible-history.com.

3. Josephus, *Josephus, Complete Works*, trans. William Whiston (Grand Rapids, Michigan: Kregal Publications, 1981), 335.

4. Randall Price, *The Stones Cry Out: What Archeology Reveals About the Truth of the Bible*, 198.

5. Charles F. Pfeiffer, Howard F. Vos, and John Rea, *Wycliffe Bible Encyclopedia, Vol. 2*, 1452.

Lesson 6

1. John R. W, Stott, *The Message of Acts* (Downers Grove, ILL & Nottingham, England: IVP Academic, An imprint of Varsity Press, 1990), 96.

2. Charles R. Swindoll, *The Greatest Life of All, Jesus* (Thomas Nelson, Nashville, Dallas, Mexico City, Rio De Janeiro, Beijing: 2008), 193–194.

3. "A Portrait of Jesus' World-Temple Culture, From Jesus to Christ, Pharisees and Sadducees, Michael L. White, Professor of Classics and Director of the Religious Studies Program University of Texas at Austin, FRONTLINE, PBS, April 1998, pbs.org.

4. Ibid.

Lesson 8

1. John R. W. Stott, *The Message of Acts*, 109.

2. Ibid.

Lesson 9

1. John R. W. Stott, *The Message of Acts*, 116.

2. Michael Rydelnik, Michael Vanlaningham and the Faculty of Moody Bible Institute, *The Moody Bible Commentary* (Chicago: Moody Bible Publishing, 2014), 1685.
3. Ibid.

Lesson 10

1. Charles F. Pfeiffer and Everett F. Harrison, *The Wycliff Bible Commentary* (Chicago: The Moody Bible Institute, 1968), 1134.
2. Ray C. Stedman, *When the Church was Young*), 116.
3. "Deacon, Deaconess," *Baker's Evangelical Dictionary of Biblical Theology*, accessed March 29, 2020, biblestudy tools.com.
4. John F. Walvoord and Roy B. Zuck, *The Bible Knowledge Commentary, New Testament Edition*, 368.

Lesson 12

1. Eusebius, *Eusebius, The Church History,* Paul L. Maier, Translation and Commentary*, (Grand Rapids: Kregel Publications, Academic & Professional, 2007), 63–64.
2. John R. W. Stott, *The Message of Acts*, 157.
3. Randall Price, *The Stones Cry Out*, 188. As cited in the article "Second Temple Replica Discovered," Jerusalem Post, April 8, 1995.
4. John R. W. Stott, *The Message of Acts*, 158.
5. John F. Walvoord and Roy B. Zuck, *The Bible Knowledge Commentary, New* Testament, 374.
6. F. F. Bruce, *New Testament History* (New York: Galilee Book, Published by Double Day, a Division of Bantam Double Day Dell Publishing Group, 1969), 230.

AUTHOR WEBSITES
www.sedertosunday.com
(contains the full Step Into Scripture Bible Study Series)
www.thebookonbullies.com
(contains the books on bullies)
www.susankboydmft.com
(contains business and contact information)

Printed in the United States
By Bookmasters